TALKING ABOUT

Six interchurch discussion booklets based on conversations worldwide

BOOKLET ONE

A flotilla of boats: what is ecumenism?

G. R. Evans

THE CANTERBURY PRESS NORWICH

The Canterbury Press Norwich, St Mary's Works,
St Mary's Plain, Norwich, Norfolk NR3 3BH

The Canterbury Press Norwich is a publishing imprint of Hymns Ancient &
Modern Limited

ISBN 0 907547 57 5

First published 1986

© G. R. Evans

Printed in Great Britain at the
University Press, Cambridge

Introduction to the Series

So many Reports and Agreed Statements about Christian unity have been published recently that anyone who has not been following the progress of the talks can easily get lost. There are now study-guides to many of these, designed to be used by groups and individuals who want to understand and discuss the issues they raise.

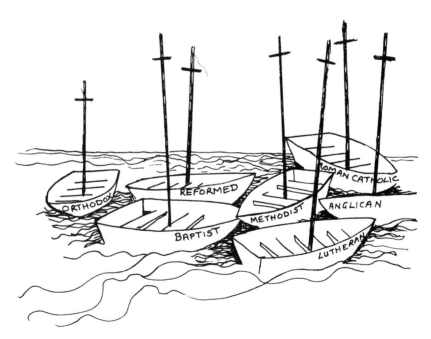

'A flotilla of boats'

The Reports show a remarkable degree of agreement, but it is still difficult to get an overall picture, simply because there *are* so many, and because they tackle their subject-matter in different orders. The first and second pamphlets in this series explain what ecumenism is about, and look at the agreement which is emerging about what the Church is. The other four try to draw together what has been agreed and present it in an easily accessible form under the main headings used in the world-wide discussions of recent decades: baptism, ministry, authority, eucharist. Practical as well as theoretical aspects are raised.

The main problem-areas which remain are gathered together as questions for groups to think about.

Each pamphlet contains quotations from the Reports, as an introduction for those who would like to go on and read the Reports for themselves.

The series can be used with study-materials available to accompany any of the reports, or as a basis for general ecumenical discussions.

J. Wilkinson and the author wish to thank the Dean and Chapter of Guildford Cathedral for permission to use photographs taken there also the Parish Council, Tregony, Nr. Truro, Cornwall; Woodstock Parish Church; Beckley Parish Church and Major Grant Datton, Porthscatho, Cornwall, for other photographs used in this series.

A sister-series, THINKING ABOUT BELIEVING, contains four further sets of six pamphlets on the Christian faith today.

A booklist

Christian communities have lately been talking to one another on several fronts. You can find an account of the way these dialogues began and a summary of what they have achieved so far in *Anglicans in Dialogue* (Church of England Board for Mission and Unity, 1984), and of others in *Growth in Unity* (see below).

Abbreviations used in these booklets

BEM   *Baptism, Eucharist and Ministry.* Faith and Order Paper 111. World Council of Churches, 1982.

ARCIC   *The Final Report of the Anglican–Roman Catholic International Commission.* SPCK/CTS, 1982.

AL   *Anglican–Lutheran Dialogue: the Report of the European Commission.* SPCK, 1983.

AR   *God's Reign and Our Unity: the Report of the Anglican–Reformed International Commission.* SPCK/St Andrew Press, 1984.

AO   *Anglican–Orthodox Dialogue: the Dublin Agreed Statement, 1984.* SPCK, 1984.

Resp.   *Towards a Church of England Response to BEM and ARCIC.* CIO, 1985.

You can buy a collection of *Reports and Agreed Statements of Ecumenical Conversations on a World Level*, ed.

H. Meyer and L. Vischer (World Council of Churches, Geneva, 1984), called *Growth in Unity*.

The Bookshop, Church House, Dean's Yard, Westminster, London SW1P 3NZ, can supply all these by post, or your local bookshop can get them for you, if you want to read the Reports for yourself.

Some study-guides

Butler, C. *The Theology of Vatican II*. Darton, Longman and Todd, 1981.

Coventry, J. *Reconciling*. SCM, 1985.

Lazareth, W. *Growing Together in Baptism, Eucharist and Ministry*. WCC, 1982.

Santer, M. *A Receptive Church: the Challenge of BEM and ARCIC*. Education and Community Division of the Diocese of London, 1985.

1. 'A flotilla of boats': what is ecumenism?

'A flotilla of boats'

The churches sometimes look like 'a flotilla of boats among which each person is free to choose the most attractive' (AR, 14). You may be in a Church of England boat, or a Methodist boat, or a Baptist boat. You may be a Roman Catholic. You may be a member of the United Reformed Church. You may be Greek Orthodox.

How did you come to be in your particular boat?

How did other members of the group join their churches?

Has anyone changed from one 'boat' to another? Why?

What is ecumenism?

St Paul draws a picture of all Christians as a single

body. All its parts are knitted together by joints and ligaments. It moves and lives and grows as a single being, and its Head is Christ himself (Col. 2. 19).

We know that that ideal was not always achieved even at the very beginning. Jesus' disciples had disagreements while he was with them, travelling and teaching (Mark 9. 34; Luke 9. 46, 22. 24). St Paul's two letters to the Corinthians were written to try to settle arguments and heal divisions. But those failures did not make it less clear that there ought to be unity among Christians. If anything, they encouraged Paul to think out more fully what unity meant and set it in the context of God's plan for the world as Jesus himself had done.

Jesus prayed that his disciples, and those who were to believe in him because of their preaching, might be 'all one'. He wanted them to be drawn into that unity which he himself shared with the Father. 'May they be in us, just as you are in me and I am in you. May they be one' (John 17. 21).

He acted on that prayer by making a reconciliation between man and God in his death on the Cross (Eph. 2. 16), and he did so in accordance with his Father's will and plan for the universe (Col. 1. 20). He actually brought about the unity he had prayed for; it is a reality which can never be destroyed. It is what man was created for and it underlies the fabric of the universe.

But it has to be worked out as a reality in the lives

of the individuals who make up the Church. Jesus taught his disciples to love and serve one another and to be patient and tolerant. St Paul repeated his teaching in all his letters, and so did Peter and James and John. Yet at best the Church in the world has been a provisional embodiment of the purpose God is working out for man. Christians constantly shatter Christ's body into fragments (1 Corinthians 1. 13). They fail to get on with one another both at local level (squabbles over the running of a bazaar) and in forming break-away groups ('we are the true Church').

The ecumenical movement is a search for unity. It seeks to bring together divided Christians and to work out the reality of Christian union with God in the world. It is as important and central as that. If Christians are not at one with one another they cannot be at one with Christ.

So the Church is one great ship, not a fleet of little boats.

What are we aiming at?

A community of faith, so that we can recognise that we are all confessing one catholic and apostolic faith. Unity by understatement is not enough. We want to find not the lowest common denominator but a real common base of faith.

Common celebration of our faith in worship and above all in Holy Communion.

The Pope and the Archbishop of Canterbury together

Common structures, so that we can work together in the world effectively as a single organisation.

These are the three things the World Council of Churches has picked out as essential for a visible unity of all the churches.

This does not mean that we are trying to arrive at a rigidly uniform set of beliefs. Unity in essential faith gives freedom for many ways of expressing it.

A necessary basis for the reconciliation of the churches is that the churches should have confidence in one another that they hold the same faith. This does not mean there ought to be a rigid uniformity but rather a unity in the Tradition at the level of faith which allows for a rich and proper diversity in traditions.

Resp. 120

On the one hand, a plurality of theological interpretations, of forms of worship, and even of disciplinary rules, is or ought to be a source of richness. On the other hand, the diversities need to be held together in unity if centrifugal forces are not to become disruptive, whether in faith or order.

Resp. 219

Do you have friends you feel close to even though they do not share all your opinions? What differences of opinion would make it difficult to call someone your friend?

What can we learn from the experience of human friendship about the

differences of opinion which can be contained in one Christian com-
munion? Are there differences which seem to you to justify division?

If any members of your group point to differences which seem to them
important you might like to bear them in mind during your discussions
and see whether they are resolved as you go along.

You can see from the New Testament that there
were tensions and differences of opinion in the earliest
Christian communities, some of them very sharp and
divisive indeed (read 1 Corinthians 1. 11–17).

Some of these differences were the result of personal
rivalries; some were differences in understanding of the
faith. These two things are not always as distinct as you
might expect. When we identify ourselves with a group
or a leader we tend to identify ourselves with a set of
opinions too. Children form rival gangs and jeer
accusations at each other. You may be able to think of
adult equivalents. Our sense of identity easily becomes
tied up with our sense of belonging. We feel safe with
our own group and fearful of others, and then we
attribute to others opinions not merely different from
our own, but which are often gross distortions.

That feeling is stronger still if the loyalty of generations
has been firmly with one church or another. In different
parts of the world Roman Catholic or Protestant Christians have suffered oppression, social disadvantage,
political difficulties, disabilities in getting jobs, even

danger to life for their faith over the centuries. Northern Ireland shows how hard it is to forget.

It is not easy, when so much has been invested in hostility for so long, to accept that the issues for which people fought and suffered and died do not matter now, or were the result of misunderstanding in the first place.

A Roman Catholic priest and a Presbyterian minister in a town in Northern Ireland shook hands as a friendly gesture for Christmas. The Presbyterian minister's family was jostled in the local supermarket. His children were shouted at at school. His wife was ignored by her neighbours. He had to leave.

Have you experienced prejudice – either prejudice you have felt against others or prejudice against you?

Have you felt a barrier of any kind between you and other people?

Where is reconciliation most needed in your life? In your community?

If we were not already divided, would we think our differences were a good enough reason to form separate churches?

(There are often bigger differences of opinion between Christians in a single denomination or local church than between Christians of different denominations. What differences have you noticed in your own congregation?)

Once we are separated, differences we could live with in our own community become part of a story we tell about others and ourselves, so that we can see where we stand. It is like making a map. What are you assuming about other Christians and about yourselves without really thinking about it?

Do we try to justify our divisions by thinking of them as matters of principle, or even saying that we are defending the Gospel itself?

Response and reception

It is not enough for theologians and Church leaders to make agreements. Their work must have a much wider effect, reaching out to the whole Church, before unity can become a reality.

There will be an 'official response' as the synods and other 'authoritative organs' of the Churches decide whether to accept the Reports and Agreed Statements as a basis for pressing forward to unity. That is already beginning, and it can go ahead quite quickly.

But although synods and councils can speak as representatives of the Church and meetings of bishops can speak for their clergy and people, they are not themselves the Church. Much more important is the process of 'reception' by which gradually the 'mind of the Church' is made up. All Christians play a part in that process (Resp. 17–21).

It is long and far-reaching. The whole Christian

community absorbs what has been said, digests it and modifies it, bringing new insights and understandings to it with the help of the Holy Spirit.

When you discuss the questions of ecumenism, formally or informally, you are taking part in the process of reception, and everything your group or you as an individual can send to the representatives who speak for your Church (to the diocesan synod, for example, or your bishop), is furthering the process of reception.

(There is more about Reception in the pamphlet *On Whose Authority?*)

Groups set up in a climate of hope and enthusiasm to try to reach agreement on the points of difference in opinion between Roman Catholics and Anglicans, between Anglicans and the Reformed Churches and so on, are now producing their reports, statements of agreements reached, pointers to the way forward. They are documents which bear out the hope which launched the discussions. On the face of it, it looks as though many long-standing problems are in sight of solution, and reconciliations may be possible.

But new difficulties are beginning to appear.

If you take a stand on an issue of principle and quarrel with your friends rather than give way, and as a result you live in estrangement from them for many years, you will have strange feelings if it turns out in the end that it was all (or 95 %) a misunderstanding and you need not have quarrelled at all. That will be equally true whether the misunderstanding was your fault or theirs, or a misunderstanding on both sides.

It is natural to try to justify what must otherwise seem a pity and a waste, if not a disaster. There are calls for apologies. If the other side has come to see that it put things wrongly or in language which obscured agreement ought it not now to say so and apologise? In any case, can perhaps four hundred years of estrangement simply be forgotten? Is the stream not hopelessly polluted by all those years of error? There are demands for adjustments of language. We cannot really recognise our faith as ours if it is not expressed in our own familiar way.

There are accusations of misrepresentation. (The agreement now before us may be in words to which both sides can agree, but is this not mere papering over the cracks? Surely each side is simply understanding the words in a different way?)

There are doubts about the substance of what has been agreed. (If agreement has been reached so readily, that may be because the real problem has not been understood.)

There are doubts about the importance of what has been agreed. (Any statement which the other side can conscientiously accept must be inadequate.)

More destructive to ecumenical endeavour perhaps than this strutting and posturing and these accusations of false emphasis is a lingering mistrust and suspicion. (The other side must be insincere in claiming to agree with us. The group which reached agreement must be made up of members too stupid to understand the implications of what they are saying. Or the group must be over-clever, determined to present a united front by cheating with words.)

Obstacles

(Or the group must have been packed with members chosen because they could reach agreement, but who are not really representative of the views of the two sides.)

All these comments have been made in response to the publication of the agreed statements and reports.

It is a promising sign that these reservations are unnecessary, that the reports and statements agree very well with one another. The world-wide ecumenical endeavour is reaching consensus; everywhere there is convergence.

Some ecumenically minded people tried to heal the divisions in the sixteenth century. One sixteenth-century Protestant called them

pretended and perfidious intermeddlers, who imagine they can admirably adjust religious differences by simply adorning their too gross corruptions with attractive colours. The actual state of things compels them to confess that the vile errors and abuses of Popery have so far prevailed as to render a Reformation absolutely necessary: but they are unwilling that the filth of this... marsh be stirred; they only desire to conceal its impurities.

When we compare the fear and hatred of this with the signs of mutual love between Christians today, it seems absurd to speak of disappointment with the progress which has been made. We have come a very long way indeed towards unity already.

So

We must *want* to be reconciled, or we can easily keep thinking up more difficulties to be settled.

We have to *trust* the other Christians we talk to to be honest in their wish to explore reconciliation with us.

We have to *listen* to one another, or we shall not understand why other Christians think as they do.

We must be *patient*.

Some schemes of full organic unity have been tried and failed. 'Plans for organic union between Anglican and Reformed churches which at one time seemed very promising have collapsed in Nigeria, Ghana, Sri Lanka, the Sudan, Canada, Australia and New Zealand...Proposals for covenanting in England and New Zealand have failed, and those in South Africa have suffered a serious setback' (AR, 4).

Perhaps the most important lesson to be learned from these disappointments is the need for a slow, gradual approach, for patience in unravelling disagreements, some of which have lasted for hundreds of years. (AR, 2)

Find out what you can about the history of your denomination. How did it come into existence? What did it stand for?

What is special about it today? Compare notes with other members of the group who belong to different denominations.

You may find it helpful to set aside a meeting to do this before you go on to the other booklets.

Clearing the field

Obstacle race

Certain topics have lain about the field of battle to trip up attempts at reconciliation ever since the wars of the sixteenth century. For Christians of different denominations each of them seems a major obstacle to unity.

As a way of shifting them, you might like to take one or more of these questions as a focus of further study. Talk to local Christians. Make some enquiries. Do a survey, perhaps. Try to get the picture as clear as possible.

(1) *Misunderstandings Anglicans and other Protestants may have about Roman Catholics*

(*a*) '*Roman Catholic services are different.*' In most Roman Catholic parishes the Sunday Mass is so like an ordinary parish Communion in a Church of England church that it is easy for an Anglican to follow it. Go to a service yourself if you can, to see; or you may be able to listen to a radio broadcast. The order of service in both cases is that of the early Christian communities turned into modern English. You will find that the balance of 'word and sacrament' (see Pamphlet VI) is familiar too, with a greater emphasis on Bible reading and preaching than Anglicans and some Protestants sometimes expect to find in a Roman Catholic Church.

If you go to Mass, would you like to be able to receive Communion with the others? In some countries there would be no objection if you did.

(b) *The respect Roman Catholics feel for the Blessed Virgin Mary and the Saints.* Protestants at the Reformation were afraid that a love and respect was being given to the Virgin Mary and the saints which should be given only to God and that that prevented people from seeing clearly the uniqueness and completeness of what Christ did for them in his life, death and resurrection.

Can the lives of good men and women help us understand better how God reaches out to us and how we can respond? Have you known such people yourself? Talk to Roman Catholic friends about what Mary means to them.

(c) *Confession.* Some Protestants as much as Roman Catholics like to confess their sins to a priest. It is not that God will not listen to them directly, but Jesus gave his apostles authority to forgive sins in his name, and for many people it is a help to talk to a trusted confessor and to hear him pronounce God's forgiveness in the name of the Church.

What do you think are the advantages and disadvantages of confessing in the privacy of your own heart and confessing to a priest?

(d) '*Roman Catholics are not allowed freedom of conscience.*' People with widely different opinions on all sorts of moral and religious questions are Roman Catholics. The Church seeks to express through its councils and through the words of the Pope what the body of the faithful believe. (You can go into this further in the booklet *On whose Authority?*)

(2) *Misunderstandings Roman Catholics may have about Anglicans or other Protestants*

(*a*) *Anglicans have different beliefs.* The Catholic faith enshrined in the Creeds is the faith of the Church of England.

(*b*) *The Eucharist does not have an important place in the Anglican Church.* In most parishes the weekly parish Communion is the main act of worship in the community, and many practising Anglicans communicate each week.

(*c*) *The Church of England was founded by Henry VIII and it has been under the government of the state ever since.* The Church of England has now effectively won self-government in spiritual matters.

(*d*) *The Church of England began in the sixteenth century.* Anglicans see their Church as continuous with the Church founded in the British Isles by St Columba and St Augustine of Canterbury a thousand years before the Reformation.

If your group, or some members of it, would like to take your study of these questions further and try to get a clear picture of Roman Catholic and Anglican teaching as a whole, you may find it helpful to set up a workshop on the work of the Second Vatican Council. J. Coventry's book *Reconciling* tackles the topics of interchurch marriages, sin and reconciliation, good and evil, praying, as well as the subjects covered in these pamplets; and C. Butler's *The Theology of Vatican II* would make a good guide too. Both can be bought cheaply in paperback.

In what ways did the reformers anticipate the thinking of Vatican II? How would you explain the Church of England's idea of itself to Roman Catholic friends?